For all those who were left behind
For all those who were not forgotten

◆ UNCOVERING ◆
AFRICAN
BURIAL GROUNDS

Kathryn Wesgate

Enslow
PUBLISHING

Please visit our website, www.enslow.com. For a free color catalog of all our hi̶g̶
books, call toll free 1-800-398-2504 or fax 1-877-980-4454.

Cataloging-in-Publication Data
Names: Wesgate, Kathryn.
Title: Uncovering African burial grounds / Kathryn Wesgate.
Description: New York : Enslow Publishing, 2023. | Series: History under cover | Includes glossary and index.
Identifiers: ISBN 9781978528741 (pbk.) | ISBN 9781978528765 (library bound) | ISBN 9781978528758 (6pack) | ISBN 9781978528772 (ebook)
Subjects: LCSH: African Burial Ground (New York, N.Y.)–Juvenile literature.
Classification: LCC F128.9.N4 2023 | DDC 363.7'509747–dc23

Published in 2023 by
Enslow Publishing
29 East 21st Street
New York, NY 10010

Portions of this work were originally authored by Therese M. Shea and published as *The African Burial Ground*. All new material this edition authored by Kathryn Wesgate.

Designer: Leslie Taylor
Editor: Kate Mikoley

Photo credits: Cover, p. 29 Carol M. Highsmith/LOC.com.; series art (scrolls) Magenta10/Shutterstock.com, series art (back cover leather texture) levan828/Shutterstock.com; series art (front cover books) RMMPPhotography/Shutterstock.com; series art (title font) MagicPics/Shutterstock.com; series art (ripped inside pgs) kaczor58/Shutterstock.com; p. 4 Commons.wikimedia.org; p. 5 Mario Suriani/APimages.com; p. 7 Sendo Serra/Shutterstock.com; p. 8 Commons.wikimedia.org; pp. 9, 10, 22, 24 Bebeto Matthews/APimages.com; p. 11 (top) Eric Glenn/Shutterstock.com; p. 11 (middle) Elnur/Shutterstock.com; p. 12 Lebrecht Music & Arts/Alamy.com; p. 13 The Eno collection of New York City views/Digital Public Library of America-dp.la; p. 14 IanDagnall Computing/Alamy.com; p. 15 Ilya Rab/Shutterstock.com; p. 15 (inset) Morphart Creation/Shutterstock.com; p. 16 The Picture Art Collection/Alamy.com; p. 17 North Wind Picture Archives/Alamy.com; p. 18 FLHC 5/Alamy.com; p. 19 1776 map/Commons.wikimedia.org; p. 20 Balfore Archive Images/Alamy.com; p. 21 (inside Museum) Commons.wikimedia.org; p. 21 (inset, aerial view) Commons.wikimedia.org; p. 23 Miljan Mladenovic/Shutterstock.com; p. 25 Mike Derer/APimages.com; p. 26 (monument) Commons.wikimedia.org; p. 27 (monument detail) Commons.wikimedia.org; pp. 28/29 (timeline art) K3Star/Shutterstock.com.

Printed in the United States of America

Some of the images in this book illustrate individuals who are models. The depictions do not imply actual situations or events.

CPSIA compliance information: Batch #CSENS23: For further information, contact Enslow Publishing, New York, New York, at 1-800-398-2504.

Find us on 󰋙 󰋐

Contents

Words in the glossary appear in bold or highlighted type the first time they are used in the text.

Uncovering History

In 1991, one of the most important archaeological discoveries of the 20th century was made in New York City. While preparing for the construction of a new federal office building in a hectic part of the city, a skeleton was found. Further **excavation** exposed another skeleton, and another, and then another. Altogether, the bones of more than 400 men, women, and children were exhumed, or unearthed. Investigations revealed the bones belonged to

Africans who lived during the 17th and 18th centuries. This area of New York had been a burial ground set aside for both free and enslaved Africans during colonial times.

Today, this location is known as the African Burial Ground. It shows us a lot about what life was like in colonial New York for both free and enslaved Africans.

~ Preparing to Build ~

Before a building is constructed, an environmental impact study is often done. Professionals study how the building might affect the people, animals, and plant life surrounding it. Another part of the study looks into the history of the site. Historical maps indicated that the plot on which the federal building was to be built had been a burial ground. However, it was thought that previous construction projects would have "obliterated any remains." Crews learned this was untrue when they uncovered the first body below the corner of Broadway and Reade Street in Lower Manhattan.

Studying the Remains

People knew that much could be learned from studying the remains. Once removed, the bones were brought to a nearby college. Then, the Cobb Laboratory in Washington, DC, was chosen to study them. This respected research institution is connected to Howard University, a historically Black school.

Human remains can reveal much about what a person's life was like, including how they ate. For example, scientists examined the teeth of the people found in the African Burial Ground. Faults in the teeth were evidence of a poor diet. Comparing these teeth to the teeth of Africans who remained in Africa their whole life revealed that the people found in the burial ground were more likely to have suffered from **malnutrition**. This was likely a result of poor diets and unhealthy living conditions.

~ Lots of Lead ~

Many of the bones studied from the burial ground had something in common: very high levels of lead. Experts found that the longer the person had lived in New York, the higher the lead levels in their bones tended to be. Lead poisoning can result in low energy, small appetite, headaches, slow body growth, hearing loss, and other health problems. It's especially harmful to children. While there's no way of knowing for sure where the lead came from, likely possibilities include certain drinks and containers used to store food.

Each human skeleton found at the site tells a story about that person's life and the world they lived in.

The People Behind the Bones

This sculpture is based on scientific recreations of what three of the people whose skeletons were exhumed may have looked like.

Studying human remains can help us get to know the people they belonged to. Learning about the bones in the African Burial Ground helped us find and tell some of their stories.

Scientists recorded each exhumed skeleton's identifying features and condition. Each skeleton was given a number. For example, "Burial 254" was the remains of a child believed to be between 3 and 6 years old. A piece of silver jewelry thought to be an earring or a piece of a necklace was found with the child.

"Burial 205" was the skeleton of a young woman with more fractures, or broken bones, than any of the other skeletons examined. She had shattered bones in her arms, legs, backbone, skull, and other places. Scientists don't know if these were from a terrible accident or a violent attack.

Photographs of some of the unearthed remains can be viewed at the African Burial Ground National Monument Visitor Center in New York City.

~ Learn Their Stories ~

"Burial 25" was a woman in her early 20s. A musket ball in her rib cage revealed that her death was violent. Scientists believe the ball was fired at her back. She was either running away, or her attacker surprised her. Broken bones in her face indicate that she was struck. New bone growth suggests she lived several more days before dying.

Another person, "Burial 259," might have been a woman dressed in men's clothing. She may have been disguising herself to get hired for certain kinds of work or to escape her enslaver.

9

Anthropologists and other scientists from the African Burial Ground Project made many shocking discoveries. One of the biggest was that half of the Africans whose remains were found and studied didn't even live to become teenagers. Others lived only a short time in the colony before they died. Undoubtedly, their hard lives had much to do with this. Their skeletons reflected a life of hardship: injured and broken bones tell of being overworked—or even worked to death.

Many people don't think of New York as having had many enslaved people. However, enslaved Africans were in fact forced to do many kinds of labor in the busy seaport. The discovery of the burial ground brought new attention to the role of enslaved Africans in the growth and building of colonial New York.

Today, people still remember those buried at the African Burial Ground in New York City.

Many people found it important for Black scientists to lead the exhumation and study of the remains. This is part of the reason why Howard University was chosen to be the location of study for the project.

~ All Sorts of Scientists ~

Many kinds of scientists were involved in unearthing and examining the skeletal remains found at New York City's African Burial Ground. Anthropologists are scientists who study humans, their origins, and their ways of life, both past and present. Archaeologists focus on studying past human life by examining bones, tools, and other objects. Other types of scientists involved in the African Burial Ground Project included geneticists and chemists.

Slavery in New York

History books sometimes make it seem as though slavery was only a problem in the American South. However, people were enslaved in the North too. In fact, enslaved Africans were a major presence in New York.

The Dutch first established a trading post that they called New Amsterdam in 1626 on the tip of the island that's now Manhattan. It became part of the

Dutch colony of New Netherland. The Dutch West India Company brought enslaved people from the Caribbean for building projects and to work in the fur trade. In 1655, the first enslaved people directly from Africa were brought to New Amsterdam.

This image shows the first auction of enslaved people in New Amsterdam in 1655.

NOVUM AMSTERODAMUM

This image shows the view of New Amsterdam from the south in 1671. *Novum Amsterodamum* is Latin for New Amsterdam.

Much labor was involved in building a colony. Land was cleared for houses, and docks were needed for ships. Enslaved people were forced to do much of this work.

~ Few Rights ~

Enslaved people may have made up as much as 40 percent of the population of New Netherland. While enslaved people in general had very few rights, those under Dutch rule in the colony had some that enslaved people in other places didn't. Their lives were still extremely difficult, but they could marry, work for themselves when not working for their owners, and own some property. They could also sue whites. There are records of an enslaved man named Anthony Portuguese suing a white businessman in 1638 after the businessman's dog hurt Anthony's pig. Perhaps even more surprising was the fact that Anthony won.

In 1644, some enslaved people in the area were given what was referred to as "half-freedom" and were allowed to farm north of New Amsterdam. They had **petitioned** for their freedom because they had performed forced labor for years and said they had been promised freedom. While they did receive some freedom, it came with conditions. In return for their "half-freedom," they agreed to share some of their grain and livestock. They also promised to work at times for the West India Company.

New Netherland was conquered by England in 1664 and shortly after became the British colony of New York. New Amsterdam, now New York City,

grew into a busy commercial center. By 1700, the city had almost 5,000 residents. By 1730, at least 15 percent of the residents were enslaved Africans.

New York was named for James II, the duke of York and later king of England. He is shown here.

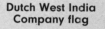

Dutch West India
Company flag

The Dutch West India Company was modeled after the Dutch East India Company, its more-successful counterpart. This ship is a recreation of the Dutch East India Company's ship, the *Amsterdam*.

~ The Dutch West India Company ~

New Netherland was the second colony to bring enslaved people to what is now the United States. The first was Virginia. However, unlike Virginia and other colonies, those first enslaved in New Netherland were not enslaved by individuals or families. They were enslaved by a business partly funded by the Dutch government. The Dutch West India Company, also known simply as the West India Company, was a Dutch trading company formed in 1621. In its day, it had even more power than companies such as Microsoft and General Motors have today.

15

With English rule, the treatment of enslaved people was harsher. They had fewer rights than under the Dutch. For example, no more than three Africans were allowed to meet in public. Enslaved Africans also had **curfews**. They weren't allowed to attend funerals after dark, which was a big part of funeral practices

Enslaved people were viewed by their enslavers as property to be bought and sold. This is a bill from such a sale made in 1785.

from West Africa. These laws were a response to fears of **rebellions**. The British also made it harder for enslaved people to be freed.

In the early 1700s, a slave market opened in Manhattan. Enslaved people were brought on ships from Africa, some younger than 13 years old. By the end of the 18th century, nearly 80 percent of Black people in New York City and nearby Westchester County were enslaved.

This image shows a slave market on the waterfront of New York City.

~ Rebellions—or Not? ~

Slave rebellions were ways in which enslaved people fought for their freedom. They included actions such as raiding and attacking. During an uprising in New York City in 1712, 23 enslaved people set fire to a building, attacked several white people, and ran away. They were later captured and killed.

In 1741, fires in New York City were blamed on enslaved Black people. Their accuser, an indentured servant, was promised her freedom for naming the wrongdoers. Several enslaved people were burned at the stake. Many historians believe the accuser was lying.

The Burial Ground's Land

In early New York City, neither enslaved Africans nor free Blacks were allowed to be buried in cemeteries with white people. In fact, they couldn't even be buried within the city. In 1673, a Dutch woman named Sara Van Borsum permitted some land she owned outside the city to become a burial ground for Africans.

We can tell that enslaved people had funeral services similar to colonists of the time from how they were buried. They were placed in wooden **coffins** with arms folded or placed at their sides. Sometimes, items such as coins and beads were placed in coffins too. The coffin was positioned in the ground so the head was facing west, a Christian tradition. As the burial ground became crowded, coffins were buried on top of coffins.

This image shows what the African Burial Ground may have looked like when it was in use.

This map shows a plan of New York City from 1776. The burial ground was located near the area labeled "Fresh Water."

~ Sara Van Borsum ~

While historians don't know everything about Sara Van Borsum, they do know some facts. Her stepfather, a minister, was known for supporting the education of Black children and for opposing wars with Native Americans.

Sara herself was a translator who received the burial ground land for helping the government communicate with Native Americans. She also received a large amount of land in New Jersey from Native Americans. One might assume by her actions that Sara was against slavery. However, that is not true. She herself enslaved at least six people.

The African Burial Ground closed in 1794. The next year, the African Society, a group established by free African Americans, opened a new cemetery for Black people in the city.

By the time the African Burial Ground closed, the city had greatly expanded. Pressure was put on "unused" sites such as cemeteries to be used for construction. In 1795, the African Burial Ground was divided up and sold. Since it was located in a ravine, it took about 25 feet (7.6 m) of fill to level it. Over the years, buildings were built, torn down, and built again. When excavation began in 1991 for the new federal building, the site of the African Burial Ground was just a parking lot. No one expected the remains to still be found at the site.

While it was known the area had once been a burial ground, experts thought the years of building would have destroyed any remains. Workers were surprised when they started finding skeletons.

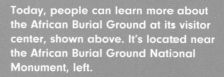

Today, people can learn more about the African Burial Ground at its visitor center, shown above. It's located near the African Burial Ground National Monument, left.

~ The First Non-Native New Yorker ~

The first non-native person to live in what is now Manhattan was a man named Jan (or Juan) Rodrigues. He was a free Black sailor from Santo Domingo in the Dominican Republic. His mother was African and his father was Portuguese. He arrived with a trading voyage in 1613. Soon, he learned the language of the Lenape people who lived there. When the others he arrived with got back on the ship to the Netherlands, Rodrigues stayed behind. He opened a trading post and later helped the Dutch trade with the Native Americans.

What to Do with the Remains?

Many people didn't want the remains that were rediscovered to be removed. They felt that exhuming the bodies and rebuilding over the site disrespected the memories of the people buried there. When Howard University took control of the excavation and research, officials promised the public that the site would be handled with reverence.

So what happened with the plans for the 34-story federal building that began the excavation in the first place? It was decided that the tower of the building would be built, but not the pavilion over the graves. Further, any new building in the burial ground area would require special permission. Still, many felt more needed to be done to recognize this special place. In 1993, the African Burial Ground was declared a National Historic Landmark.

Today, Bryant Park is one New York City's most well-known parks. In the 1800s, it was a burial ground for the city's poor residents.

~ History Below Your Feet ~

It may seem unusual that a cemetery could be hidden for hundreds of years. However, the African Burial Ground isn't the only final resting place to be covered, paved, and forgotten about while New York City expanded. According to the Parks Department, more than 50 of the city's parks are on lands that were once used for burials. Union Square, Washington Square Park, and Bryant Park are just a few examples. In other places where construction took place, remains were either moved or left where they were, forever buried under buildings and streets.

A Final Memorial

For more than a decade, the bones that had been removed from the African Burial Ground were studied. Finally, in 2003, each of the 419 human skeletal remains were prepared for reburial. Each skeleton was placed into a hand-carved wooden coffin made in the African country of Ghana.

In September 2003, the remains began their journey from Washington, DC, back to New York. Four people were chosen to symbolize those buried in the African Burial Ground: an adult male, an adult female, a male child, and a female child. They stopped in cities along the way where enslaved

Africans had worked. The remains were set into their final resting place at the African Burial Ground Memorial Site on October 4, 2003. In 2006, the African Burial Ground was named a U.S. National Monument, making it protected by the government.

Throughout the journey from Washington, DC, to New York, many people gathered to pay their respects to those being laid to rest.

~ Marking and Honoring the Graves ~

Because of African traditions in other places, anthropologists believe the original graves of the African Burial Ground were marked. Stone slabs have been found near some graves. Others were marked with wooden posts or boards connected to the head or foot of coffins. Loved ones likely held ceremonies to honor those laid to rest and continued to visit the burial ground following the ceremonies. Many believed the reburial was an important part of respecting and remembering those the remains belonged to.

A Place to Remember

In 2007, a memorial designed by **architect** Rodney Leon was completed. It's a tribute to the past, present, and future generations of Africans and African Americans. Writing on a memorial wall explains that the memorial is:

> *"For all those who were lost*
> *For all those who were stolen*
> *For all those who were left behind*
> *For all those who are not forgotten."*

There is also a visitor center for the African Burial Ground. Located on the ground floor of the Ted Weiss Federal Building, the tower built on the grounds, visitors can read about Africans' role in early New York as well as the story of the burial ground, past and present. Models of the unearthed findings, a movie, and various exhibits can also be viewed at the visitor center.

If you go to New York City, you can see the outdoor memorial at the **intersection** of African Burial Ground Way, which was formerly Elk Street, and Duane Street.

~ At the Monument ~

The African Burial Ground National Monument includes a gathering space for ceremonies and a chamber for quiet reflection. The Wall of Remembrance describes events involving the African Burial Ground's creation. Leon included many African symbols in the memorial as well. Visitors can follow a curving path that leads through a map of Africa, Europe, and North and South America. The center of the spiral is West Africa, where the ancestors of many African New Yorkers were from.

Today, people visit the monument to honor those buried there and to remember the role enslaved people played in building New York City.

The African Burial Ground helps us understand the past, but it can also help us learn about the present. Upon the discovery of the bones, it became important to the African American community of New York City to take ownership of the unearthing and research of those in the cemetery. These were their ancestors. Studying the remains and creating the memorials have helped people understand parts of history that otherwise may have been lost.

The 1991 discovery reminded many that the city of New York only became the great city that it is today because of the labors of African residents, whether enslaved, "half-free," or liberated. When the African Burial Ground National Monument was **dedicated** in 2007, it was the first to be dedicated to Africans of early New York.

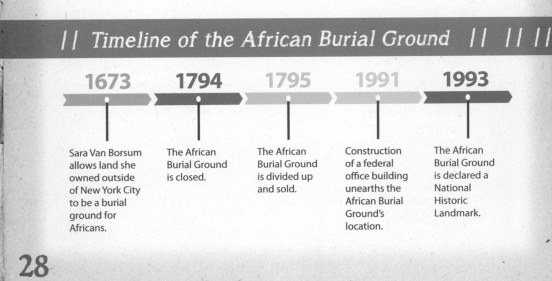

|| Timeline of the African Burial Ground || || ||

1673	1794	1795	1991	1993
Sara Van Borsum allows land she owned outside of New York City to be a burial ground for Africans.	The African Burial Ground is closed.	The African Burial Ground is divided up and sold.	Construction of a federal office building unearths the African Burial Ground's location.	The African Burial Ground is declared a National Historic Landmark.

African Burial Ground
National Monument

2003	2006	2007	2010
The bones removed from the African Burial Ground are reburied.	The African Burial Ground is named a U.S. National Monument.	The memorial by architect Rodney Leon is finished.	The African Burial Ground National Monument Visitor Center opens.

GLOSSARY

architect: a person who designs and guides a plan, project, or building

coffin: a box in which a dead person is buried

curfew: an order or law that requires people to be indoors after a certain time at night

dedicate: to officially open a place for honoring or remembering something

excavation: the act or process of digging and removing earth in order to find something

geneticist: a scientist who studies genetics, or things related to genes

indentured servant: one who signs a contract agreeing to work for a set period of time in exchange for passage to America

intersection: the spot where two or more streets meet or cross each other

malnutrition: the unhealthy condition that results from not eating enough food or not eating enough healthy food

musket: a type of long gun that was used by soldiers before the invention of the rifle

obliterate: to destroy something completely so that nothing is left

petition: to ask for something in a formal way, typically when a group of people come together to ask for something in writing

rebellion: an effort by many people to cause change, often by the use of protest or violence

FOR MORE INFORMATION

Books

Albee, Sarah. *Accidental Archaeologists*. New York, NY: Scholastic Press, 2020.

Uhl, Xina M. *A Primary Source Investigation of Slavery*. New York, NY: Rosen Central, 2019.

Websites

The African Burial Ground
www.gsa.gov/portal/content/101077
Read about the discovery that started it all.

African Burial Ground National Monument
www.nps.gov/afbg/index.htm
Find out more about the burial ground including how to visit it.

Please visit our website, www.enslow.com. For a free color catalog of all our high-quality books, call toll free 1-800-398-2504 or fax 1-877-980-4454.

Cataloging-in-Publication Data

Names: Wesgate, Kathryn.
Title: Uncovering depots of the Underground Railroad / Kathryn Wesgate.
Description: New York : Enslow Publishing, 2023. | Series: History under cover | Includes glossary and index.
Identifiers: ISBN 9781978528789 (pbk.) | ISBN 9781978528802 (library bound) | ISBN 9781978528796 (6pack) | ISBN 9781978528819 (ebook)
Subjects: LCSH: Underground Railroad–Juvenile literature. | Fugitive slaves–United States–History–19th century-Juvenile literature.
Classification: LCC E450.W4226 2023 | DDC 973.7'115–dc23

Published in 2023 by
Enslow Publishing
29 East 21st Street
New York, NY 10010

Portions of this work were originally authored by Caroline Kennon and published as *Depots of the Underground Railroad*. All new material this edition authored by Kathryn Wesgate.

Designer: Leslie Taylor
Editor: Kate Mikoley

Photo credits: Cover, p. 8 Zack Frank/Shutterstock.com; series art (scrolls) Magenta10/Shutterstock.com; series art (back cover leather texture) levan828/Shutterstock.com; series art (front cover books) RMMPPhotography/Shutterstock.com; series art (title font) MagicPics/Shutterstock.com; series art (ripped inside pgs) kaczor58/Shutterstock.com; p. 4 North Wind Picture Archives/Alamy.com; p. 5 Courtesy of the Metropolitan Museum of Art, New York; p. 6 Everett Collection/BridgemanImages.com; p. 7 Heidi Besen/Shutterstock.com; p. 9 https://commons.wikimedia.org/wiki/File:Undergroundrailroadsmall2.jpg; p. 10 Associated Press/APimages.com; p. 11 (bottom) North Wind Picture Archives/Alamy.com; p. 11 (top) Everett Collection/Shutterstock.com; p. 12 https://commons.wikimedia.org/wiki/File:Harriet_Tubman_Civil_War_Woodcut.jpg; p. 13 (left) Everett Collection/Shutterstock.com; p. 13 (right)/https://commons.wikimedia.org/wiki/File:Harriet_Tubman_late_in_life.jpg; p. 14 Chronicle/Alamy.com; p. 15 Everett Collection/Shutterstock.com; p. 16 karenfoleyphotography/Shutterstock.com; p. 17 Charles Phelps Cushing/Alamy.com; p. 18 https://commons.wikimedia.org/wiki/File:The_Dr._Nathan_M._Thomas_House.jpg; p. 19 BD Images/Shutterstock.com; p. 20 Associated Press/APimages.com; p. 21 ttps://commons.wikimedia.org/wiki/File:Lewelling_Salem_IA.JPG; p. 22 https://commons.wikimedia.org/wiki/File:Milton_House_Milton_Wisconsin_October_2011.jpg; p. 23 (left) Randy Duchaine/Alamy.com; p. 23 (right) Randy Duchaine/Alamy.com; p. 24 Historic Images/Alamy.com; p. 25 (bottom) Everett Collection/Shutterstock.com; p. 25 (top) https://commons.wikimedia.org/wiki/File:Gerrit_Smith_house,_Peterboro,_New_York.jpg; p. 26 Frederick Douglass, head-and-shoulders portrait, facing left., [Between 1870 and 1900] Photograph/loc.gov; p. 27 Cindy Hopkins/Alamy.com; p. 29 Everett Collection/Shutterstock.com; p. 29 Auchara Phuangsitthi/Shutterstock.com.

Printed in the United States of America

Some of the images in this book illustrate individuals who are models. The depictions do not imply actual situations or events.

CPSIA compliance information: Batch #CSENS23: For further information, contact Enslow Publishing, New York, New York, at 1-800-398-2504.

Find us on

Contents

Words in the glossary appear in bold or highlighted type the first time they are used in the text.

The Railroad That Wasn't a Railroad

By the mid-1800s, newspapers in New York City, Boston, Massachusetts, and other American cities were using the term "Underground Railroad" to describe how some enslaved people mysteriously escaped their enslavers. Several stories exist for how the term came about. One says it happened in 1831, when an enslaved Kentucky man named Tice Davids swam across the Ohio River toward freedom. According to the story, Davids's enslaver said he must have "gone off on an underground railroad." Other stories tell of enslaved people discussing an "underground railroad to Boston."

Of course, the Underground Railroad wasn't an actual railroad. It was a massive effort by enslaved and free people alike to secretly bring thousands of enslaved people to freedom in the North. For many, the final destination was Canada, often called the "Promised Land."

Artists often used real experiences of people on the Underground Railroad to shape their work. This piece shows a man escaping slavery by crossing the Ohio River, like Tice Davids may have done.

This painting is by Theodor Kaufmann, a soldier who fought for the North in the American Civil War. Some art experts think this work shows the lack of a clear route to liberty for enslaved people trying to escape.

~ Who Ran the Railroad? ~

Some say that an organized system to help people escape enslavement may have begun as early as the end of the 18th century. In 1786, George Washington complained that one of the people he enslaved had run away with help from a "society of Quakers, formed for such purposes." The Quakers were a religious group who were strongly and publicly against slavery. In the 1800s, the Quakers were a major part of the Underground Railroad. However, it was free Northern Black Americans who were the main force in running the Underground Railroad.

Looking for Freedom

In the 18th and 19th centuries, enslavement was common in America. Those enslaved were mostly descendants of Africans. After the American Revolution, northern states such as Pennsylvania and New York began to abolish, or end, slavery. Southern states such as Alabama and Mississippi retained it. The economy in the South largely depended on the forced labor of enslaved people.

Wanting freedom, many enslaved people in the South attempted to escape north. They often required help getting there. This help took the shape of a hidden network of people and places leading to freedom. As the term "Underground Railroad" became popular for the network, so did other terms relating to trains.

"Conductors," "passengers," and "stations" were all used to describe the individuals and locations in the Underground Railroad. Secret codes helped get people to freedom.

The conductor was responsible for moving those on the run from one depot, or station, to the next. Harriet Tubman was one of the most famous conductors.

Today, statues all over the country honor the important work Harriet Tubman and many others did on the Underground Railroad. This one is in Boston, Massachusetts.

~ Enslavement in the North ~

History books often make it seem as though slavery was only an issue in the South. While Northern states did end slavery before the South, it's important to note that slavery existed throughout America. In many states, even after laws were passed to free enslaved people, the practice remained for a time. For example, New York passed an **emancipation** law in 1799, but many enslaved people in the state weren't officially freed until 1827. **Census** records even show that some were still enslaved until at least 1830.

On the Underground Railroad, depots and stations were the homes and businesses where those escaping enslavement would stop to hide, sleep, and eat. Those who owned these locations and welcomed escapees were called stationmasters. Individuals who contributed money or supplies were called stockholders.

The Harriet Tubman National Historical Park in Auburn, New York, lets visitors see where Tubman lived for a time.

A majority of the individuals helping to get people to freedom were Black. Most of the people involved only knew of the local efforts to help people escape slavery and not of the overall operation. The Underground Railroad succeeded because of the hard work of these individual people at the local level, not necessarily because of a larger system of routes.

Only a few thousand enslaved people escaped each year. However, enslavers considered these people to be their stolen property. Escapees—and those who helped them—became a big concern for enslavers.

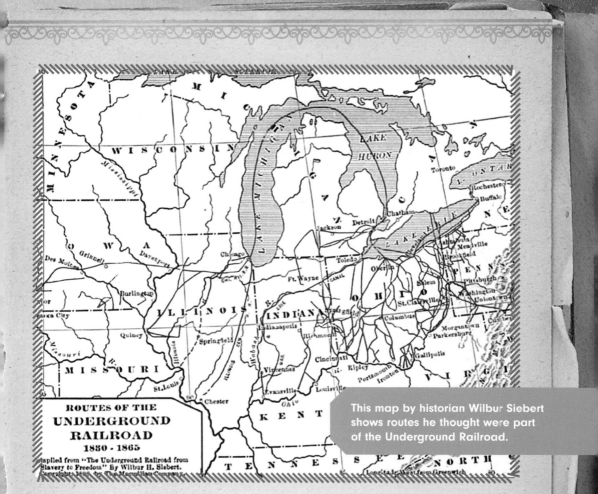

ROUTES OF THE
UNDERGROUND
RAILROAD
1830 - 1865
Compiled from "The Underground Railroad from Slavery to Freedom" By Wilbur H. Siebert.
Copyright 1898 by The Macmillan Company.

This map by historian Wilbur Siebert shows routes he thought were part of the Underground Railroad.

~ Routing the Railroad ~

Many think both **abolitionists** and enslavers **exaggerated** the organization of the Underground Railroad to help their causes. In 1898, historian Wilbur H. Siebert published detailed maps of the supposed routes of the Underground Railroad. Despite this, historians now believe that it wasn't actually so neatly structured. Historian Eric Foner stated that the Underground Railroad was a "series of local networks . . . which together helped a substantial number of fugitives reach safety in the free states and Canada." While most Underground Railroad routes headed north, others led south to Mexico and the Caribbean.

Escaping to freedom was a difficult and high-risk task. Escapees left in the middle of the night, sometimes led by a conductor pretending to also be enslaved. They often traveled 10 or 20 miles (16 or 32 km) until they reached a depot where they could rest safely. Then they waited until the next stop could be notified and prepared for them. It was illegal for anyone to help enslaved people in any way once they had escaped, so conductors, stationmasters, and stockholders were all at risk too.

In 1850, the Fugitive Slave Act was passed. It required that all runaways be returned to their

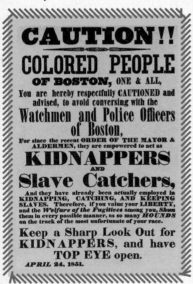

enslavers. People who helped the escapees were supposed to be punished. Even formerly enslaved people who had escaped to free states had to be hidden due to the act.

This 1851 poster from Boston, Massachusetts, warned of slave catchers. The outdated term "colored people" refers to Black people. Today the term is generally considered offensive.

~ Disguising Runaways ~

Even though the Underground Railroad wasn't a real railroad, sometimes those running away did have to use trains to travel longer distances. They also had to use boats to cross water. When they used these forms of transportation, they couldn't look like they were enslaved. If they did, people would know they were fleeing. Instead, they needed to look like free Black people. This meant wearing clothes that weren't worn or ragged. Both transportation and new clothing cost money. Funds were often donated by generous individuals or raised by antislavery groups.

Get to Know Harriet Tubman

Conductors and stationmasters were important in helping freedom seekers. Probably the most well-known conductor was Harriet Tubman. She's known to have helped rescue about 70 people from slavery and likely gave instructions to about 70 more who continued to freedom on their own. Tubman told Frederick Douglass, an escaped enslaved man who became a famous abolitionist and writer, that she "never lost a single passenger" on her travels using the Underground Railroad.

Tubman was born into slavery in Maryland around 1820. In 1849, afraid that she would be sold, she

left on foot and walked to Pennsylvania, stopping along the Underground Railroad on the way. The next year, she went back to get her sister and sister's children. On her third trip, she rescued her brother. She wanted to continue helping others escape.

Before becoming a conductor, Tubman used the Underground Railroad for her own escape.

Frederick Douglass (left) said of Harriet Tubman (above), "I know of no one who has willingly encountered more perils and hardships to serve our enslaved people."

~ More About Harriet ~

Harriet Tubman was nicknamed "Moses," after the Hebrew leader in Judaism and Christianity who led his people out of slavery. In addition to her work on the Underground Railroad, Tubman also worked as a **Union** spy during the American Civil War (1861–1865). All those trips back and forth between the North and the South leading people to freedom made her very familiar with the land. She worked with a group of other formerly enslaved people and reported on the movement of the **Confederate** troops, sometimes posing as an enslaved person herself.

Many Underground Railroad depots were privately owned homes, but some were public buildings. These depots could be found all over the country. One was the Plymouth Church of the Pilgrims in Brooklyn, New York. An Underground Railroad conductor named Charles B. Ray brought passengers to the Plymouth Church from Manhattan. The freedom seekers probably hid in the basement.

Though it only opened in 1847, the Plymouth Church of the Pilgrims was one of the most important places for the antislavery movement.

The minister of this church was Henry Ward Beecher. He was the brother of the author Harriet Beecher Stowe, who wrote the antislavery novel *Uncle Tom's Cabin*. Beecher was famous himself for his antislavery preaching. Every week about 2,500 people attended Plymouth Church

to hear Beecher's sermons, which were also printed and passed around. Beecher encouraged people to resist slavery, disobey the Fugitive Slave Act, and become active in the Underground Railroad.

Henry Ward Beecher is pictured here with his sister, Harriet Beecher Stowe.

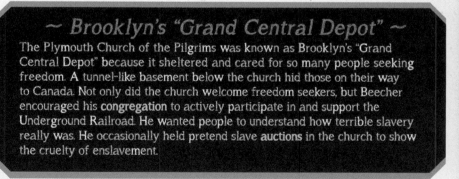

~ Brooklyn's "Grand Central Depot" ~

The Plymouth Church of the Pilgrims was known as Brooklyn's "Grand Central Depot" because it sheltered and cared for so many people seeking freedom. A tunnel-like basement below the church hid those on their way to Canada. Not only did the church welcome freedom seekers, but Beecher encouraged his **congregation** to actively participate in and support the Underground Railroad. He wanted people to understand how terrible slavery really was. He occasionally held pretend slave **auctions** in the church to show the cruelty of enslavement.

One of the only Union-controlled military buildings in the South during the Civil War was Fort Monroe in Virginia. This military base also played a role in helping some escape slavery.

In 1861, people enslaved by Confederate colonel Charles Mallory were working on Confederate military projects near the fort. They heard they were to be moved to North Carolina, further into Confederate territory. So, on May 23, they sought safety within Fort Monroe. General Benjamin F. Butler refused to send the people back to their enslaver, as the Fugitive Slave Act required. He said they were "**contraband** of war."

In August 1861, Congress passed the Confiscation Act, allowing the Union to confiscate, or take, any property from the Confederates. This meant they could take enslaved people, as they were considered property.

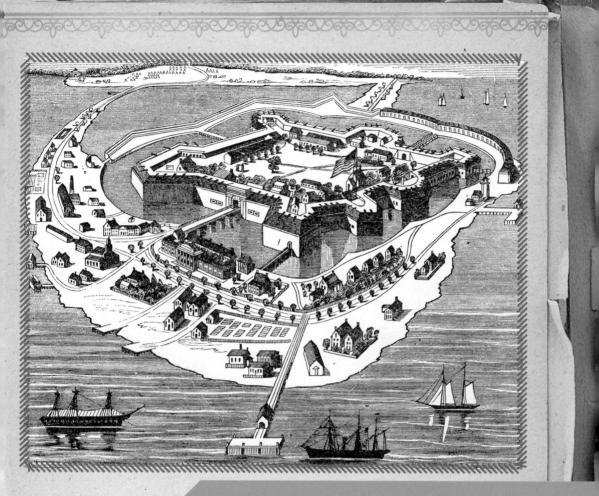

Fort Monroe was sometimes known as the "Freedom Fortress."

~ Life at the Fort ~

Once the Confiscation Act was passed, thousands of freedom seekers began traveling to Fort Monroe. By the time the war ended in 1865, more than 10,000 had come to the fort for safety. The formerly enslaved worked to earn their stay. They completed labor such as building roads. This led some to argue that those who escaped to Fort Monroe weren't actually free at all but had only changed enslavers. Harriet Tubman also worked at Fort Monroe for a time. She worked as a nurse, cooked, and did laundry.

The Thomas House

The first doctor in Kalamazoo County, Michigan, was also a big part of the antislavery movement in the state. His name was Nathan Thomas. His strong antislavery views led him to start a newspaper devoted to antislavery news. Between the years 1840 and 1860, Thomas and his wife Pamela Brown Thomas aided the Underground Railroad. Their home in Michigan was a depot for between 1,000 and 1,500 freedom seekers who were eventually taken to Canada by way of Detroit.

The Thomas House

The couple provided food, mended clothing, and treated the injuries of escapees. Their work was done at night and in secret, but neighbors knew about it and even helped with food. Pamela Brown Thomas's memoirs, or writings about her life, have informed much of what we know about their involvement in the Underground Railroad.

Michigan, being so close to Canada, played an important role in the Underground Railroad. Today, the Gateway to Freedom International Memorial in Detroit reminds visitors of that role.

~ On the Quaker Line ~

The Thomases were Quakers. Escapees who came through the area where the Thomases lived were said to be "on the Quaker Line." This was the nickname for a series of Underground Railroad depots in Michigan. John Cross, a Quaker from Indiana, is thought to have been one of the organizers of the line. He also **recruited** local "conductors" like the Thomases.

Other Quakers helped along the line too. Zachariah Shugart often brought freedom seekers to the Thomas home. Later, Thomas would bring them to another Quaker named Erastus Hussey.

19

Henderson Lewelling moved to Salem, Iowa, in 1837 with his brother. The two planned to open a general store. Salem was the first Quaker community in the state of Iowa. There, Lewelling helped establish the Abolition Friends Monthly Meeting. This meeting was attended by Quakers who not only opposed slavery, but also wanted to help those seeking freedom from it. In addition to being the home of the monthly Abolition Friends meetings, Lewelling's house was also an Underground Railroad depot, welcoming the formerly enslaved on their journey to freedom.

Hiding places, such as trapdoors, were built into the house. A tunnel under the house connected

Freedom seekers were often hidden below floorboards with trapdoors such as this one at the Lewelling Quaker Museum.

to a basement fireplace, allowing those who were seeking freedom to slip away easily when people looking for them arrived.

The Henderson Lewelling House was an important depot that helped many on their journey to freedom. Today it is a museum.

~ From Missouri to Salem ~

Salem is only 25 miles (40 km) from Missouri, a state that allowed slavery. A well-known enslaver from Missouri, Ruel Daggs, came to Lewelling's house with armed men and threatened the residents and the entire town of Salem. Still, he was unsuccessful in getting those who had escaped his enslavement back. According to the *Iowa Journal of History and Politics*, Daggs "finally realized the difficulty of holding slaves so near the free State of Iowa and **contemplated** selling his slaves south so that he would be free from the necessity of keeping a constant guard on valuable property."

Joseph Goodrich's Milton House

Members of another religion that stood passionately against slavery were Seventh Day Baptists. Joseph Goodrich was born in 1800 into a Seventh Day Baptist family in Massachusetts. In 1838, he traveled to Wisconsin with other Seventh Day Baptists and founded the town of Milton. It was located near Rock River, a **tributary** of the Mississippi River—and a route for enslaved people escaping to Canada.

Goodrich built an inn called the Milton House around 1845. The inn was also a refuge for those who had escaped enslavement. To avoid being seen by inn guests, freedom seekers entered a log cabin behind the inn. A trapdoor into the cabin's basement led to a tunnel that ran to the inn's basement. There, Goodrich supplied food and beds for the escaped.

Part of the Milton House is shaped like a hexagon. This means it has six sides.

Part of the original Milton House cabin still stands today. Escapees used a trapdoor inside the cabin to enter the tunnel (left) that led to the basement of the inn.

~ A Crawl to Freedom ~

The tunnel that ran from the Goodrich cabin to the inn was built after the inn was completed. It had been dug into the earth and was only 3 to 5 feet (0.9 to 1.5 m) high. The channel was so small that those using it would have had to crawl on their hands and knees in total darkness for 45 feet (13.7 m) from the basement of the cabin to the basement of the Milton House. In the 1950s, the tunnel was made larger for visitors of the house, which is now a museum..

Gerrit Smith

In 1835, 600 antislavery supporters gathered for a conference at a church in Utica, New York. Abolitionist Gerrit Smith was one of them. A large group of **rioters** stormed the building during this gathering, forcing the meeting to end. Smith offered to host the meeting on his own estate in Peterboro, New York. These events led to Smith serving as the president of the New York Anti-Slavery Society between 1836 and 1839. He encouraged abolitionists to help people escape slavery.

In the 1840s and 1850s, Smith was a stationmaster in the Underground Railroad too. His estate was well known as a safe place for passengers on their way to Canada. Smith also helped free Black people start lives locally by either giving away or selling land at a low price.

Gerrit Smith, shown here, was cousins with famous women's rights leader Elizabeth Cady Stanton.

The Gerrit Smith House was destroyed by fire in 1936. However, much of the estate remains and can be visited today.

AM I NOT A MAN AND A BROTHER?

~ A Gift of Wealth ~

Gerrit Smith was a generous man, often giving money to abolitionists for expenses. It's estimated that he gave away over $8 million in his lifetime—which in today's money would be more than $1 billion! He sometimes purchased enslaved people directly from their enslavers in order to free them. Some thought he shouldn't give money to enslavers, but rather give it to organizations that fought slavery. Smith also gave money to John Brown, who would raid a weapons storehouse in Harpers Ferry, Virginia, in 1859 in a failed attempt to start a slave rebellion.

Nathan and Mary Johnson

Nathan and Mary "Polly" Johnson made some of the most important contributions to the Underground Railroad in Massachusetts. They were free Black Quakers who lived in New Bedford, Massachusetts. There, they owned a whole block of properties and helped many freedom seekers to escape slavery. The most well-known person they helped was probably abolitionist Frederick Douglass. In fact, the Johnson house was Douglass's first home after he escaped from slavery in 1838.

After Nathan left for the California Gold Rush in 1849, Polly housed at least one more fugitive on their journey to seek freedom from slavery. Polly helped pay for and maintain their properties in New Bedford by selling candy and cakes. Today, the Johnson house is a National Historic Landmark and is owned by the New Bedford Historical Society.

Frederick Douglass

This was the first home Frederick Douglass lived in after escaping enslavement. For safety, those who escaped slavery often changed their names. Nathan Johnson helped Frederick decide on the last name "Douglass."

~ The Community of New Bedford ~

In 1853, New Bedford had a higher population of African Americans than any other city in the Northeast. Almost 30 percent of these residents reported that they had been born in the South. The number of people living there who had escaped from slavery ranged from 300 to 700. Some New Bedford schools and neighborhoods were **integrated**, which was unusual at that time. Additionally, Massachusetts was one of only five states that allowed Black people to vote at the time. This attracted many free Black people.

More to Learn

The Underground Railroad was a huge effort by many people. This book only names a few of the depots we know about today. It also only mentions some of the brave individuals who risked their lives escaping slavery or helping others do so before slavery was finally abolished in 1865.

Many depots no longer stand, and some probably weren't recorded at all. Their routes and the people who acted as conductors and stationmasters on them remain a secret. But because of these depots and people, thousands of formerly enslaved people found freedom.

|| Timeline of the Underground Railroad || || ||

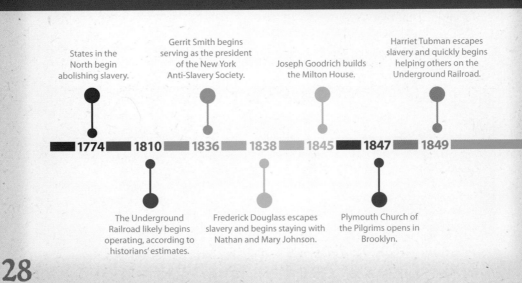

States in the North begin abolishing slavery.

Gerrit Smith begins serving as the president of the New York Anti-Slavery Society.

Joseph Goodrich builds the Milton House.

Harriet Tubman escapes slavery and quickly begins helping others on the Underground Railroad.

1774 **1810** **1836** **1838** **1845** **1847** **1849**

The Underground Railroad likely begins operating, according to historians' estimates.

Frederick Douglass escapes slavery and begins staying with Nathan and Mary Johnson.

Plymouth Church of the Pilgrims opens in Brooklyn.

Today, many places that were depots along the Underground Railroad are museums or historic sites. Visiting these places can help you learn much more about this important part of history. Ask an adult to help you find out if one is near where you live.

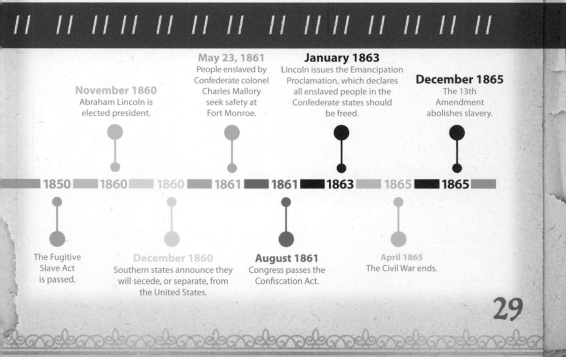

~ Public Support ~

Some historians estimate that about 100,000 people escaped slavery using the Underground Railroad. Not all abolitionists kept their work with the Underground Railroad so secret. In fact, many were quite public with their views and actions despite the consequences. The governor of New York from 1839 to 1842, William Seward (left), openly supported the Underground Railroad and kept escapees hidden in his basement while serving as a senator. Some northern towns and cities even openly held bake sales to raise money to help the Underground Railroad.

May 23, 1861
People enslaved by Confederate colonel Charles Mallory seek safety at Fort Monroe.

January 1863
Lincoln issues the Emancipation Proclamation, which declares all enslaved people in the Confederate states should be freed.

November 1860
Abraham Lincoln is elected president.

December 1865
The 13th Amendment abolishes slavery.

1850 ▦ 1860 ▦ 1860 ▦ 1861 ▦ 1861 ▦ **1863** ▦ 1865 ▦ **1865** ▦

The Fugitive Slave Act is passed.

December 1860
Southern states announce they will secede, or separate, from the United States.

August 1861
Congress passes the Confiscation Act.

April 1865
The Civil War ends.

GLOSSARY

abolitionist: one who fought to end slavery

auction: a public sale at which things are sold to people who offer to pay the most

census: the official process of counting the number of things or people and collecting information about them

Confederate: relating to the Confederate States of America, the states that left the United States during the American Civil War

congregation: an assembly or gathering of people, especially for a religious service

contemplate: to think deeply or carefully about

contraband: things that are brought into or out of a country illegally

emancipation: the act of freeing from the restraint, control, or power of another, usually referring to the freeing of enslaved people

exaggerate: to think of or describe something as larger or greater than it really is

integrate: to give races equal membership in something

recruit: to persuade someone to join some activity

rioter: one who behaves in a violent or uncontrolled way

tributary: a stream that flows into a larger stream or river or into a lake

Union: the Northern states during the period of the American Civil War